I0491663

THROUGH

THE

TUNNEL

Helping Start-ups Survive and

Grow from Humble Beginnings

By

Dr Ukadike Ake

i

© Copyright 2020 by Dr. Ukadike Ake – All rights reserved.

It is not legal to reproduce, duplicate or transmit any part of this document in either electronic means or printed format. Recording of this publication is strictly prohibited.

This book is dedicated to:

To my parents who have helped me from the beginning Chief G. U. Ake and Mrs Christiana Ake, you taught me to open my heart to learning.

My siblings, who gave me a fun filled childhood.

My Uncles and Aunties, your discipline and love has helped to shape me.

And to all my teachers, you poured knowledge into an empty vessel.

They say it takes a village to raise a child, I had a village and half.

Table of Contents

Introduction

This book is the second in my 'Ground breaker' series, aimed at helping entrepreneurs, managers and business leaders, to start and run successful organizations. The first book, 'Hit the Ground Running', discussed the processes involved in getting the enterprise started including planning, seeking for funding and recruitment. This book covers concepts that ensure the firm survives the early days and blossom into what the entrepreneur has envisioned.

Many small businesses do not survive their first two years. The reason is that they are faced with a myriad of challenges which include funding, taxes and levies, government and industry regulations, administrative and personnel issues and the list goes on.

This book attempts to simplify some of the puzzles facing the modern entrepreneur, by providing knowledge in plain terms on several key issues that start-ups have to deal with. The topics in this book cover the hard and soft skills required to lead an organization.

The celebrated football coach, Sir Alex Ferguson, once scoffed at commentators that said he had to plan for one match at a time. Ferguson reminded them that it's still the manager's job to plan for the matches to be played after the next one and the next one after that, and so forth. The business leader has to cater for the long term of the firm, as well as the day-to-day operations i.e. he or she has to think about strategy and tactics, just like a General at war or a coach of a sports team.

This book discusses concepts that deal with strategy like deciding on marketing approaches and keeping savings, as well as day-to-day tactics, such as handling difficult employees and dealing with crisis.

The process of writing this book, has allowed me to draw from my personal experiences in several business ventures cutting across various sectors from construction to leasing to hospitality, spanning a period of twenty-five years. This is in addition to my academic pursuits in the field of management with qualifications including an MBA and a Doctorate in Business Administration. The ability to combine practical and theoretical knowledge

2

allows me to discuss these leadership/entrepreneurial/management issues from a rich and insightful point of view.

I hope this book will help entrepreneurs and leaders to run long surviving and successful organizations that brings joy to them and those that work with them. It is my earnest wish that by reading this book, entrepreneurs will avoid some of the mistakes I have made during my time as a budding businessperson.

Chapter One – Thinking about Strategy

Thinking about Strategy.

"Success without strategy is like winning a jackpot, that comes only once in a lifetime. Therefore, to replicate success, you need strategy."

Charles Okeibunor.

When starting, most small business owners don't involve strategic thinking in the running of their businesses. They set up shop and take things one day at a time. Most times these entrepreneurs change tactic on whims, or they try to do everything and be everything at the same time. This is neither smart nor sustainable for small businesses, because it affects profitability, planning and allocation of resources.

Most businesses operate in competitive environments and strategy helps to set them apart from the rest of the field. Michael Porter, the management guru, argues that competitive strategy is about being different[1], he posits that strategy is about intentionally carrying out "a different set of activities to deliver a unique mix of values." Strategy is all about gaining competitive advantage, it's not enough to be effective in what you're doing. For the business to thrive, you have to deliver the product to those that require it and are willing to pay value for it, without getting drowned out by the multitude of similar providers.

Porter also argues that strategy is about 'trade-offs', choosing what not to do, so you can focus and be better on the area(s) you decide to operate in. I was once involved in leasing heavy equipment for construction. We started with earth-moving equipment such as bulldozers and pay-loaders, and because we failed to have a thorough discussion on strategies, we made the mistake of following the trend as at the period in time.

Back then, many people were going into purchasing tipper trucks for leasing and we just dove right in. We didn't want to be left out, but this was out of our core business area and it didn't match what we were already doing. The kinds of spare parts were different, the maintenance specialists were different, and the kinds of customers were also different. Dealing with the truck drivers and much more frequent maintenance issues, started taking up a lot of our time and resources.

Essentially, this was a distraction from the areas we had already built competence over the years. At the end of the day, we decided to sell off these trucks at far less prices than we had purchased them. Our failure to craft and execute a well-thought out strategy, ended up in expensive mistakes.

Having a strategy helps the entrepreneur answer the following questions:

- What are the specific problems I'm trying to solve?

- Who are my customers and what are their peculiarities in terms of desires, location, behaviours etc.?

- What do I need to meet the needs/wants of these customers?

- What should I focus on and what can I trade-off to best satisfy these customers?

- How does my operation affect the service to my customers?

- How do I reach my customers?

The answers to the questions above will lead business to decide on the type of strategy to use.

Types of Strategies

Different strategies have been developed by management experts, including strategies that look at competing globally or locally and others tailored to large or small corporations.

Generic strategies exist in the literature termed as marketing strategies, competitive strategies and so on and so forth. Marketing strategies can be classified according to the following: Mass marketing,

Segmentation, and Niche marketing[2]. While, the broad competitive strategies include low-cost provider, broad differentiation, best-cost provider, focused (market niche) based on low costs, and focused (market niche) based on differentiation[3].

In this chapter, I will focus on the marketing strategies. But before we dive into these marketing strategies, I would like to discuss the most common form of competitive strategy entrepreneurs adopt, which is the lowest cost provider strategy. This can be effective, when a firm is able to operate in such a manner that brings down its production costs compared to the costs of its competitors.

However, most times entrepreneurs who have not achieved this level of operational efficiency still try to offer lower prices than their rivals, in order to snatch customers away. This approach is likely to fail in the long run, when costs begin to outrun profits and the business is forced to either reduce the quality of the product or raise prices.

It might be better to strive for a best-cost provider strategy. This approach attempts to provide more value for money by surpassing customer expectation in areas such as quality, features, performance and service when compared to other competitors.

The other generic competitive strategies, differentiation and niche are similar to those covered under marketing strategies i.e. segmentation and niche marketing.

Marketing Strategies

I believe that small businesses should pay close attention to marketing strategies because they help identify potential target markets and hence, assists entrepreneurs in tailoring their operations towards target customers. These strategies are referred to as marketing strategies but we must remember, marketing is all about identifying customer needs and delivering value to the customers. Thus, these strategies could be seen as competitive strategies as well.

The marketing strategies I will discuss below include those tailored for mass marketing, segmentation/differentiation and niche marketing as developed by the authors Kotler and Keller[2].

Mass Marketing

This is when a seller undertakes mass production, mass distribution and mass promotion of one product for all buyers. You can call it a one-size-fits-all approach. This is what products like Coca-Cola and Indomie noodles attempted to do for years and were quite successful at it.

Mass marketing has the likelihood to potentially create an extensive market, leading to lower costs and consequently, translating to lower prices and higher margins[2]. However, critics of mass marketing argue that today's market has become too fragmented and the lightning pace of growth of the advertising and media channels make it too costly to reach a mass audience[2]. This is especially true for small companies; hence they have to pick a target market and gear their promotions and other efforts towards these potential customers.

Segment Marketing

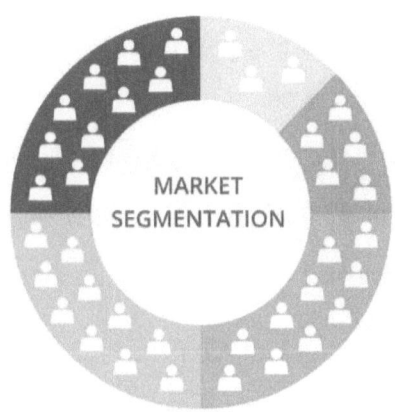

A market segment "consists of a group of consumers who share a similar set of needs and wants.[2]" The marketer is saddled with the responsibility of identifying the segments and deciding which segment or segments to deal with.

Market segmentation can be done on several bases:

1. Geographic – nations, states, regions, counties, cities and neighbourhoods.

2. Demographic – Age, family size, gender, income, occupation, education, religion, race, nationality etc.

3. Psychographic – Psychographics is the science of combining psychology and demographics to better predict consumers. In this type of segmentation, consumers are divided based on psychological/personality traits, lifestyle or values.

4. Behavioural Segmentation – customers are divided into groups based on their knowledge

of the product and their attitude or response towards the product.

The marketer can decide to adopt a flexible differentiation (segmentation) strategy consisting of a naked solution, comprising of the product and service elements that are valued by all segment members. Then, the offering can include discretionary options that some segment-members value and these options can be charged for separately.

An example is the market for amateur golf equipment, where sellers offer different sizes of golf clubs at certain prices, whilst also offering 'club-fitting' services to those that require this service at additional prices.

Niche Marketing

A niche is "a more narrowly defined customer group seeking a distinctive mix of benefits[2]." Niches are identified by dividing segments further, into sub-segments. The niche market, according to corporate strategy authors Thompson, Strickland and Gamble[3], can be identified by geographical peculiarities, special product requirements or features that appeal only to the niche members.

For a niche to be attractive, it should be made up of buyers that have a detached set of needs and are willing to pay good value to the provider who best meets these needs. A niche market is relatively small but has the potential to grow in terms of profit and size and most times other competitors chose to ignore these markets due to their size. However, niche providers benefit through specialization.

An example of a niche marketer is the clothing line, High and Mighty. They cater to tall and big men, which is an area that most apparel lines don't see as profitable since their numbers are small.

Niche providers have benefited from the rise of online shops which are appreciably cheaper to set up compared to traditional 'brick-and-mortar' shops. Kotler and Keller advise potential internet niche players to aim at products that customers do not need to see and touch.

Chapter Summary/Key Takeaways

- It is important to craft a strategy before embarking on a business venture and most entrepreneurs fail to do this. Leaving them with an inability to compete against rival providers.

- Strategies that can be adopted include mass marketing that attempts to produce and market to all types of consumers. Most times, it is advisable to identify market segments and tailor products to suit the needs of these segments. Segments could be based on geography, demographics or consumer behaviour.

- Niche marketing involves identifying segments and further breaking down into sub-segments and catering to the requirements of the unique group.

The next chapter presents the important issue of taxation. I make the argument about why we should plan for taxes from an early stage and what kinds of taxes an entrepreneur is expected to pay.

Chapter Two - Tax: The Other Certainty

Tax: The Other Certainty.

"Whereas I was blind, now I see"
John 9:25.

There goes a story in the Bible about how Jesus was tested by the Pharisees and scribes on the payment of taxes. They initially tried to flatter Jesus, calling him a man of knowledge and integrity before posing the question on whether the Jews should pay tax to the Roman ruler. They were hoping for Jesus to oppose this unpopular levy, so they could hand him over to the Roman governor, Pontius Pilate. The story goes that Jesus asked for a coin and asked whose head was on the coin, to which they responded that it was Caesar's head. Then Jesus gave the famous advice, "Render therefore to Caesar the things that are Caesar's, and to God the things that are God's."

At worst, taxes should be seen as necessary evils and at best, crucial to the building of societies. In the story above, Jesus' response meant that these taxes were the law of the time. Loathe it or love it, every entrepreneur must plan for taxes and have a fair knowledge of the local taxes that affect their business. A lot of people, when thinking of starting a business, are blind to taxes, this chapter is to help you gain sight.

Running a business in Nigeria is extremely difficult, the entrepreneur has so many obstacles to contend with, electricity, rent, salaries and so many other issues, and then there's tax. It is no secret that a lot of businesses do not pay their taxes in Nigeria, but one incontestable truth is that if you want to grow, as a company or businessperson, you have to pay your taxes and show evidence that you've done that.

For you to provide services to or do business with government agencies, multinational corporations and other international agencies, you must demonstrate tax compliance. What is more, to assess funds from several local or international organizations, you also have to be tax compliant, in almost all instances.

Below is a summary of the importance of understanding taxation and paying taxes as an entrepreneur.

- It helps in planning about resource allocation.

- Corporate clients require evidence of tax compliance to do business with you.

- Banks require tax compliance evidence to give out loans.

- When you are tax compliant, you don't get on the wrong side of the law and you avoid punitive actions from the government.

- You contribute to the development of the society by paying taxes.

What is a Tax?

A tax is a "charge against a citizen's person or property or activity for the support of government" (Advanced English Dictionary[4]). Taxation has always been around in Nigeria, even before the British colonials landed on our shores. The traditional rulers collected these taxes or levies in the various parts of the country. In the North, there was Zakat (a religious tax), Kudin-kasa (land tax) and Shuka-Shuka (cattle-rearing tax), while in the West, Isha-Kole (land tax) was paid to the Obas as well as other taxes. In 1903, Lord Lugard introduced the Stamp Duties Proclamation and this was the start of government participation in taxation in Nigeria.

Now we can argue on the fairness of the country's tax policies with regards to small and medium scale businesses but that's a discussion for another day. What is pertinent right now, is that you don't get into all sorts of problems because of ignorance. For most of us that aren't lawyers or accountants, the word 'tax' evokes the images of labyrinths and mazes, and we just want to ignore it. But ignorance isn't a magic password when the authorities come knocking on your doors with huge chains and mean-looking police officers.

What Taxes Should I Pay?

There are several levels of taxes applicable to Nigerian businesses: Federal, State and Local government taxes. The main taxes that apply to the average Nigerian company are: Company income tax, Education tax, Value Added tax, With-holding tax and

Personal income tax[5]. I'll attempt to make some sense regarding these taxes in the next few paragraphs.

Company Income Tax was previously payable on taxable profits at thirty (30) percent on the preceding year basis. This must be filed six (6) months after the end of the accounting year for existing companies and for newly registered companies, eighteen (18) months from the date of incorporation or six (6) months after the first accounting period, whichever comes first.

However, it is important to note that the Nigerian government has reviewed the law regarding company income tax. According to the Finance Act 2020, small businesses with turnover of less than 25 million naira are exempt from paying company income tax, while businesses with turnovers ranging from 25 million to 100 million naira will now pay 20% instead of 30%. This was done to further encourage small and medium scale businesses.

Education Tax is payable on the company's assessable profit at two (2) percent and it is normally paid alongside the company income tax.

Value Added Tax (VAT) is payable at five (5) percent on all VAT-able goods and services. VAT payment should be filed on the 21st day of the month following the transaction. There are some goods and services that are exempted from VAT and these include: medical products and services, unprocessed staple foods, educational goods and services, commercial vehicles and spare parts etc.

With Holding Tax (WHT) is an advanced payment on income tax deductible at source on specified transactions. WHT varies from 5% to 15%, based on services performed. Incorporated companies should remit WHT to the Federal Inland Revenue Service (FIRS), while individuals and unincorporated bodies are to remit to state-level Inland Revenue Services. You must request for a credit note from the body that initially deducted With Holding tax, to allow you offset this from your payable company income tax.

Personal Income Taxes (PIT) are payable on incomes of individuals including employees, partnerships and unincorporated trusts. This tax is usually paid to the state-level Internal Revenue Service. So, if you own a business that you manage and you pay yourself a salary, you are supposed to remit PIT on this salary, as well as deduct and remit PIT from your employees to the State Government.

It is essential to reiterate to the reader, that the owners of businesses registered under business names or as enterprises, are subject to Personal Income Tax, alongside the owner(s)'s earnings from other sources including, salaries from employment, dividends and interests from investments and other income earned. The owners of such enterprises/business names are also expected to serve as agents for the government by deducting and remitting PIT from its employees to the government, as well as collecting and remitting from clients, other taxes such as VAT and Withholding tax to the government. PIT is administered by the respective State Government where the individual resides.

It might also be necessary to mention the National Social Insurance Trust Fund (NSITF) contributions, where businesses with more than 5 employees are required to pay a percentage (1 percent) of their payroll towards the NSITF contributions.

There other taxes and levies that are applicable, especially at the state and local government levels, besides those presented above such as business premises levies, development levies, road taxes, radio/television levies, contributions to Industrial Training fund etc. that may be enacted by specific State laws, and mostly administered by the State / local governments or other agencies of government as well. It is important that entrepreneurs try to get aware of these.

An important advice I would give is that you consult a tax expert or accountant. These specialists could be recruited to function on an in-house basis or as an external consultant, whichever might be more affordable.

Conclusion

However, it is not all doom and gloom for the entrepreneur as there are funds available to SME's in Nigeria such as the Federal Government Special Intervention Fund for MSME's and Bank of Industry and Central Bank of Nigeria Intervention fund etc. But just as I've mentioned previously, you have to show evidence of being up to date with your taxes to assess these funds.

Getting access to these funds are never a certainty just as most things in life but the two certainties, as the Benjamin Franklin once said, are death and taxes.

Chapter summary/Key takeaways

- Taxes are levied by government on individuals, businesses and properties, and avoiding payment of taxes is criminal by law.
- Several taxes exist, which a businessperson should be aware of including: Company Income tax, withholding tax, Value Added Tax etc.

The next chapter talks about employee commitment to the organization. The factors that influence commitment are discussed and the ideas on boosting commitment are presented.

Chapter Three - Above and Beyond:
Building Employee Commitment

Above And Beyond:
Committed Employees
Are The Nectar Of Small Business.

You've put in so much money to establish your business, you've offered more money to poach qualified hands, you've sacrificed your comfort and luxuries to start what seemed at the time, a sure bet. But a year down the line, you are struggling to get others to buy into your vision. You are having to either fire employees or others are quitting unexpectedly.

The workers that are still around aren't displaying 'a sense of ownership', when it comes to the company property or even its customers, especially when you are not around. Other times, what you observe is just plain old dishonesty and stealing by those you've entrusted to help grow the business. This is what most entrepreneurs face when trying to grow their businesses. The question most ask is – how do I get workers that are committed to the business?

Improvement in employee commitment to the organization has been found to provide the following benefits inter alia:

- Increase in the performance of the firm, both in terms of financial and operational performance.

- Reduce employee turnover and absenteeism.

- Improve job satisfaction, job performance and adherence to organizational policy/strategy.

Recently, I organized an action learning sessions (ALS) with a group of entrepreneurs and managers, who all wanted answers to this same question. Over several sessions, they talked about their unique circumstances, questioned and critiqued themselves, and proffered solutions to one another. Several themes and solutions were revealed at the end of the process and the themes included communication, rewards, career path and leading by example.

I believe the outcome of the sessions could be beneficial to other entrepreneurs and thus, I would attempt to articulate these outcomes.

Communication

Ironically, some of the problems entrepreneurs face, especially when it comes to getting people to key into their visions, emanates from them. My interactions with business owners and managers revealed a common issue, the inability to effectively communicate with their team members or subordinates.

During the AL sessions, I asked these executives to gather feedback from their subordinates about their management style and most of them came back with similar responses. They were told that they don't take opinions from team members, they don't share their plans, or they don't show enough concern for what others were going through. My advice is to organize weekly, monthly, quarterly and annual meetings to discuss both operational issues and overall strategies.

During these meetings, the leader should let other team members take turns speaking or presenting before them and should only interrupt to clarify issues.

Another good practice is to take your team out to non-work environments, this will allow people to let their guards down and probably reveal issues that would ordinarily remain latent. Also, we should occasionally, reveal our human sides, show empathy, get to know what others are going through in their lives.

Rewards

Creating a system that rewards performance tells employees that their contributions are acknowledged, appreciated and valued. Rewards can be financial or non-financial in nature. Financial rewards are important because besides their monetary value, they demonstrate a sense of value to the employees from management.

However, rewards should not only be financial in nature, other non-financial or intrinsic rewards are just as important. Granting more autonomy to workers, allowing participation in decision-making and introducing some variety to work tasks are important intrinsic rewards. One method, the executives in the action learning group suggested was rotating leadership responsibilities in various aspects of the organization's work or to rotate leadership in tackling specific problems.

For instance, the owner of a small hotel complained about high electricity costs because his staff members weren't being mindful of switching off appliances, when not in use. A possible solution proposed to him was to form a task force that would investigate the problem and ensure the attitude towards conserving energy in the organization changes. Leadership of such intervention committees could be rotated, and even job roles could be altered to add some variety to work tasks.

The relationships within organizations operate on the principles of social exchange and reciprocity. When individuals perceive they are being treated well and valued, they in turn reciprocate through improved commitment, better performance, and going above and beyond what their roles prescribe.

Creating Career Paths

Putting in place a system that allows workers to grow from one role to a higher one conveys a 'sense of belonging' to employees, according to the managers in the action learning group. Even small businesses should articulate a growth path for their employees, as this would represent a motivational target to inspire better performance.

Career growth, asides promotion and increase in remuneration, also involves assisting your employees to develop their professional abilities. This can be achieved through sponsoring training programmes or paying for professional exams. Another form of career development could be establishing a path for co-ownership, this is very vital in some professions like the legal sector and could be very useful in other sectors to drive commitment.

Just like rewards, managing employees' career development, is hinged on reciprocity and social exchange i.e. when employees perceive value in management actions, they in turn try to reciprocate through improved commitment, performance and going above and beyond their assigned roles.

Leading by Example

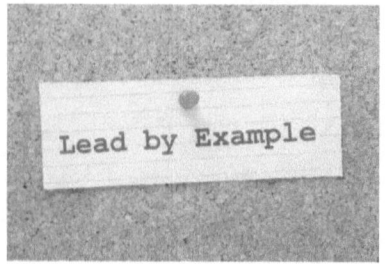

One last point that should be made is about showing example. Most entrepreneurs lack discipline in two key areas, finances and spending the needed time the business requires. Some of the managers I spoke with confessed to frequently dipping into their company finances to solve personal problems. This is very understandable, after all the point of investing in a business is to make your life more convenient but this must be done in an organized way.

What I would say next may sound a bit trite but still very relevant, you must fix a salary for yourself and this should be affordable for the business. Secondly, any borrowing must be recorded and mostly paid back, I know not all can be repaid but nine out of ten times, you need to put back your 'director's drawings'.

The other area is dedicating enough time to the venture. If you want a certain culture in your organization, you must be there to instill that culture, at least for a gestation period before your ideas take root. A lot of us allow laziness to creep in and this affects the behaviours of your team members. If you desire commitment, you must show commitment.

To achieve some of the suggestions I have presented, it might be necessary to move away from the traditional organizational structure, which is hierarchical and bureaucratic in nature, to a more fluid and participatory structure.

Chapter summary/Key takeaways

- Committed employees perform above and beyond their designated work roles.

- To enhance commitment, leaders should communicate effectively, ensure rewards are adequate, plan for career growth/development and lead by example.

In the succeeding chapter, we discuss about dealing with difficult employees in the workplace. This is a common problem in most work environments and difficult employees constitute a minority in terms of numbers but can cause serious damage to the workplace environment.

Chapter Four - Dealing with Difficult Employees

Dealing With Difficult Employees.

Conflict is common in every organization. Sometimes even healthy, especially when it brings out fresh ideas and different perspectives. But when conflict takes a negative tone, it becomes corrosive to the team spirit and a source of stress to individuals in the workplace. It is often the case that the majority of conflict in most organizations arise from the actions of a few individuals, confirming Pareto's 80/20 law i.e. the manager spends 80% of his or her time dealing with problems created or stoked by 20% of the workforce or team.

Dealing with difficult employees is often exasperating for the manager or team leader and stressful for most people in the situation. Hence, another reason why it should be dealt with effectively rather than ignored and left to fester. Managers can handle difficult employees in several ways, including actually 'managing' these employees i.e. using soft skills and training. If these don't work, another way to handle difficult team members is by employing punitive measures.

We can summarize the importance of dealing with conflicts:

- Conflicts can affect the performance of an otherwise effective team, thereby affecting product quality, customer service and overall profitability of the firm.

- Conflicts can cause stress and affect the health and wellbeing of team members.

- Dealing with conflicts effectively helps to bring more understanding, respect and can strengthen bonds amongst the team.

Moving forward, we explore the different approaches to deal with difficult team members.

The Good Bad Ones

Some employees who pose challenges might have positive sides that are valuable to the organization. Some might be hardworking and passionate about their jobs and the organization, but make bad team players or have insubordinate streaks. In other situations, some team members might just be experiencing a temporary dip in performance due to personal circumstances.

A manager should always develop the skill of listening actively to the individual team members especially those in the categories I have described above. It is essential that employees are allowed to communicate their challenges. In some cases, some empathy or probably counselling could suffice. Other instances could require giving the employee a short break from work. Also, arranging for training could go a long way to help some individuals to deal with changing workplace environments or build teamwork skills.

Conversely, some situations might call for creativity from the manager. An interesting story was narrated in the book 'The Heart of Change' by John Kotter and Dan Cohen[6]. The story talks about Joe, a hardworking but difficult employee that was stuck in the 'old ways.' Joe felt the company's products needed no modification, despite several complaints and feedback from the customers. Joe's boss wasn't willing to let go of an employee that was obviously dedicated to the company, so he decided to try out a different approach.

The employee, Joe, was compelled to spend six months working in the customer's facility as a quality inspector, while his original company continued to pay his salaries. He was explicitly told that failure wasn't an option and he did not want to fail, so he immersed himself in the job given and for the first time, he started seeing things from the customer's perspective and how certain products were not meeting the customer's needs.

After the six months, he came back to his company but this time, he was put in the role of customer representative and he became an excellent inspector, helping the company improve its products to suit the customers.

Wielding the Big Stick

The story above illustrates how managers can deal with difficult workers by thinking deeply and in this case changing responsibilities, however, it is important that punishment is also used when necessary i.e. to correct and deter negative behaviours.

Managers often utilize four main types of sanctions: informal oral warnings, formal written warnings/queries, suspension or loss of pay and dismissal. It should be highlighted that existing research has shown that supervisors who use sanctions more often, also have high performance ratings compared to those who rarely use them, according to Charles O'Reilly and Barton Weitz in their article "Managing marginal employees: The use of warnings and dismissals[7]."

Managers more often rely on the first three punitive measures (verbal warnings, written warnings and suspensions) before dismissals and this is the advisable approach in most situations. This demonstrates that a process has been followed and opportunities for the employee to change have been provided. This sends a signal to others that punitive tools are available, and the manager is not afraid to use them, moreover, such a process protects the organization from accusations of victimization or wrongful dismissal, if it comes to that.

However, when all measures previously mentioned fail or prove not to be adequate, David Freed, in an article aptly titled "One more time: Please fire marginal employees[8]", urges managers to fire marginal employees. He defines marginal employees as those with "sustained poor attitudes or performances and such a person fails to improve even when confronted with the need and tools to do so".

Freed provides several reasons why marginal employees should be dismissed, according to him, poor performers often bring down an otherwise successful team. Secondly, a manager should not retain someone he or she cannot fully support, this portends no positive outcome for the employee, team or organization. Thirdly, termination might be personally difficult, but it rejuvenates the team and invites for a fresh start. Lastly, according to Freed, marginal employees rarely improve.

Dealing with difficult or marginal employees is always a source of stress to the leader and other team members and when such issues are not dealt with properly, it has the potential to wreak havoc on the working environment and affect performance. Hence, managers need to take firm decisions on such issues.

When Relationships (Personal and Professional) Collide

There are some situations where firing someone is even more delicate and difficult. An instance is when you have a personal relationship with the difficult employee. In often cases, the personal relationship precedes the work relationship and there is the desire to preserve the bond. The management relationship expert, Charles Okeibunor suggests exploring options that preserve the personal relationship. It is important to be truthful to yourself, if the work relationship is not tenable, you have to explore ways to end it whilst maintaining the personal friendship. You can have a meeting with the employee in question and find out what he or she desires personally, in the long term and if you can assist in making that work outside the job environment, by all means help out. However, delaying the inevitable separation will only make matters worse in the workplace.

Chapter summary/Key takeaways

- For employees going through a phase, managers should try different approaches including giving short-breaks, training and empathizing.

- Managers should not shirk from using punitive measures when the situation warrants.
- Keeping marginal employees around creates a toxic environment and brings stress to co-workers.

The next chapter moves our discussion from conflict to crisis. Crisis in the organization represent a turbulent period with several serious situations confronting the corporation in a simultaneous manner. Crisis defines the future of the organization, how we respond to crisis decides if the organization will sink or swim in the aftermath.

Chapter Five - Crisis in the Organization

Crisis and change are both constantly evolving themes within organizations. Change is always an ongoing process because of the different dynamics inherent in human nature and technology. Crisis also evolves because there are other preceding situations that occur before a crisis that usually go unnoticed and other events take place after the crisis has been set in motion. In a lot of situations, change and crisis are related because so many crises occur because of failure to foresee and carry out changes.

This does not mean that all crises happen because of a failure to change. Of course, there are often unforeseen and unpreventable events, like due to a major health crisis (COVID-19) or a natural disaster (the Asian Tsunami in 2004 and Hurricane Katrina in 2005) or global financial crisis (the economic meltdown in 2008) etc.

Culture and Crisis

Crises can be differentiated into two distinct categories: the first category is unavoidable and usually caused by natural forces (acts of God) such as tornadoes or earthquakes; the second category is avoidable and is usually man-made such as corporate scandals. In this chapter, we will focus on the second category, avoidable crisis.

Avoidable crisis occurs due to the failure of organizations to carry out necessary changes. Crisis could be prevented or at least an organization could prepare itself to deal with such occurrences, if the necessary adjustments are made from the current way of doing things. These changes are ongoing rather than isolated events that occur within a defined period. These changes could be targeted at the organizational culture, work content and context, or the structure of the organization.

Dangerous Cultures

According to research, one of the common factors that has been identified in the investigation of disasters was the apparent clinging to harmful organizational beliefs, practices and the presence of toxic culture within organizations. It is important to note that organizational culture is a constantly unraveling phenomenon and for management to achieve a positive culture within its organization there must be persistent monitoring and efforts to engender the necessary culture.

Thinking about harmful organizational culture gets me thinking about the worldwide protests against police brutality I see in the news today. Worldwide protests erupted in 2020, when a video of a policeman pressing his knee on the neck of George Floyd, an African American man, for about eight minutes. This happened while other police officers watched without trying to intervene. George Floyd later died from asphyxiation, highlighting a culture of police brutality in the US, especially towards people of color.

I think the excessive use of force captured by police officers in the United States, Nigeria or any country goes beyond rogue individuals but has its roots in the systemic culture of those institutions. I am sure if you analyze how these officers are recruited and trained, you will find the core of the problem.

These institutions need to completely change their recruiting and training philosophies to come to terms with the present reality, which is that the communities they serve are better informed and expect to be served by the police and not commanded. Also, technology has evolved in such a way (with the rise of social media) that their actions are more scrutinized by the public at large.

Make Learning Internal

Field research goes further to suggest that an organization's culture affects its preparedness to respond in times of crisis. Organizations that are only concerned about their internal welfare and have little regard for their environment and human relations were found to have little structures in terms of crisis management and vice versa. Whereas, organizations that have a learning culture and do not shun past failures but rather are willing to examine and learn from past organizational failures, are able to deal with crisis better.

An example of companies trying to make changes to avoid crises, can be found in the oil/gas sector. Most of the multinational companies in this sector are beginning to invest in research on renewable energy sources because they suspect that the future of global energy lies beyond fossil fuels, which are their major sources of revenue presently.

It's Time to Listen

As supervisors, team leads, managers, business owners and leaders, we must ask ourselves – what kind of culture do we create or promote in our organizations? Do we allow our team members, subordinates, workers or followers question our decisions? Do we encourage debate or criticisms targeted towards our ideas? It is better to endure a little bruise on your pride and avoid an expensive crisis on your hands at the end of the day.

One way to encourage open exchange of ideas, is to offer a seat to someone who works in your office to report a problem or seek instructions. This relaxes the individual and removes tension from the exchange.

Secondly, try to ask the subordinate or team member their opinions, even if the final decision rests on you. It might be a well-worn statement, but two heads are *really better* than one. Lastly, don't shoot the messenger, people often respond negatively to the bearers of bad news, but we should avoid this as it might discourage early reporting of potential disasters and prevent immediate actions to be taken to nip the crisis in the bud.

When it Rains, It Pours

As the head of an organization, it is your job to handle crisis situations and you are expected to deal with such events with a positive outcome at the end. The difficulty is that crisis often occurs with multiple events, there is usually more than one serious situation that you have to deal with at the same time and this can be emotionally and mentally crippling. However, we must remember that things do not get better by running away from our troubles. Below are several suggestions on how to face such difficult situations.

Prioritize the Issues – By analyzing the problems in terms of importance helps you bring clarity to the situation. Doing this could even make the predicament less daunting and this helps you think of strategies to address the issue.

Taking One Step at a Time – Try to do things one at a time, instead of overwhelming yourself trying to take on everything at once. If possible, assign tasks to other team members, while you face the most important or urgent issue. A lot of time, managers have resources at their disposal but do not utilize these assets, because of ego or a failure to trust others.

Decide what to focus on – In most situations, you should focus on the most urgent situation, the one that can bring the whole house crashing down if not addressed. However, if you cannot do anything about the most urgent problem at the moment, then focus on the problem with the least resistance. This sounds counterintuitive, but this strategy is often very helpful. By addressing the issue with the least resistance, you are able to keep busy and build confidence when you resolve this.

Preserve Your Mental State – Don't lose your mind worrying or panicking. If you lose your head, others around you will also lose theirs, resulting in complete chaos. Find what calms you down and embrace it, for some it is through prayer, others it's by meditating, some might repeat a mantra or key phrase, while some might need someone to talk to. I'm not suggesting the 'do nothing' approach but I think it is important that you preserve your mental well-being.

Take the Risk of Negotiating – In some situations, it might be possible to bargain for better conditions than the one at hand. If you try, it might be possible to negotiate more time or better payment options, etc. Rather than just offering false promises, like saying "give me up till next week" when you know that by next week, nothing would have changed, you should be bold enough to ask for conditions you know you can meet up with.

Chapter summary/Key takeaways

- Crises can often be avoided by identifying changes to be made and executing these changes.
- The culture of the organization plays a role in avoiding and dealing with crisis.
- Have a strategy to deal with crisis, don't panic or run away.

In the next chapter, I advocate for businesses to develop a saving culture. It takes discipline to put funds aside as savings and the benefits of savings could literally save the business in times of crisis.

Chapter Six - Saving for a Rainy Day

Saving For A
Rainy Day.

In December 2019, a new strain of the coronavirus was discovered to be responsible for the deaths of many people in Wuhan, China. This caused the world to go through drastic changes and things might never return to how they were before that December in 2019.

What happened in Wuhan was something new, but many business management writers and economists have always advocated for business to keep a kitty for rainy days. Covid-19 has only brought to stark focus the dangers of not putting down savings as a business entity.

What Should Go in the Kitty

Some experts have advocated putting aside up to a third of income or sales, but the choice should depend on the peculiar situation the business finds itself in and the size of the company. What is vital is to keep aside as savings at least ten percent of your income for the unknown situation. This is difficult, when we consider so many needs that this cash can meet, especially in a growing business but we must build this discipline, otherwise a seemingly innocuous occurrence could bring the business to a grinding halt.

Phil Knight narrated in his book 'Shoe Dog'[9], how he habitually poured all his revenue into buying more inventory, always leaving nothing in the company's bank account. He got a lot of grief from his bankers and even got kicked out from a couple of banks. While this strategy worked a while for the great Phil Knight, we might not be so lucky and find that one day, all we toiled for could be jeopardized because we had no money to deploy in a time of emergency.

Benefits of Saving

Now, to the reasons why an emergency fund is necessary. In times of sudden crisis, such as one we find ourselves in with Covid-19, emergency funds will allow a business to take care of its most important assets, its workforce, at least for a reasonable period of time. When companies are able to keep paying staff salaries for a few months in a crisis situation, an immeasurable amount of goodwill and loyalty is built amongst the staff members. The team members feel valued not only for their skills but as human beings because this might be in a period where their skills cannot be deployed.

It makes me cringe when well-known brands announce pay-cuts and lay-offs immediately when faced with a crisis situation, such as the lockdown resulting from the coronavirus pandemic. There might be backstories behind some of these actions but on the surface, it smacks of insensitivity, cruelty and sometimes, poor management on the part of the leadership of these companies.

Not being able to support your workers in the aftermath of a significant event not only breeds ill-will amongst the team members but also puts the brand in a negative light in the eyes of the public.

Companies are faced with different kinds of crisis, which can be different from a health pandemic. In 2009, a driver in the US was involved in a fatal accident driving a Lexus due to an improperly installed floor mat. Following the backlash from the media, public and government, Toyota recalled millions of vehicles from the US and the rest of the world. The US auto journal, Automotive News, estimates that Toyota recalled during the period from 2009 to 2011, a total of 20.5 million vehicles[10].

After thorough investigations by the US regulators and NASA, it was found that Toyota's electronic system, that was initially blamed for several crashes, was not at fault but rather most of the accidents were caused by 'driver error'[11]. At the end, Toyota ended up losing millions of dollars and taking serious hits to its brand image.

But the question remains, if Toyota was a company that lacked tons of resources in reserve, would they have survived the recall crisis? I think not.

Another benefit of having emergency funds is the ability to carry out needed works on the business property or properties. These could include renovation works, replacements or upgrades to software that were affected by the event or that could not be carried out during normal operations because of the disruptions and inconvenience it would cause customers. This could see the business coming out even stronger than before the crisis, poised to retain customers and possibly, attract even more customers and increase sales.

Businesses that save are able to take advantage of opportunities that suddenly become available. It could be real estate or equipment that comes into the market at very attractive prices and are in the plans already. Moreover, businesses could be tested with the advent of new technology and those that have resources can adapt and adopt these new technologies.

In today's world, there are advances in artificial intelligence and telecommunications, which are changing the face of competition in most industries.

At the end of the day, having an emergency kitty is a win-win for the entrepreneur. She is able to quickly deal with issues that require immediate attention in a timely fashion. The funds deployed to keep the workers afloat, can build feelings of loyalty and increase commitment in the normative sense. Also, when the business operations are halted because of the event, renovations and upgrades can be carried out. All these will see the company's brand image boosted both internally and externally.

Chapter summary/Key takeaways

-   SMEs should put aside 10 to 30% of their revenues as savings.

- Savings help businesses respond to emergency situations.
- Savings also gives your bankers some confidence to do business with you.

Chapter Seven - Standing Out in a Crowded Room

Standing Out In A Crowded Room

If you ever visit Balogun market in Lagos, Nigeria, you would notice that a long line of stores could be selling just a particular product, say towels. In another long line, you would only find maybe, shoes. The intriguing aspect of this is that, there is hardly any means to differentiate between one trader and the other, looking at these shops from the outside.

But if you take some time to observe what goes on along any particular line of wares, it becomes more interesting. You would find that eighty percent of the buyers, purchase from two or three shops out of the tens of sellers in any particular line or section.

The scenario described above compels one to ask the question, how can a small business stand out? In this chapter we will address that question looking at the soft factors. In previous chapters we have discussed some of the hard factors that could help the entrepreneur stand out, such as marketing strategies and the likes. However, in this chapter we will try go beyond the technical aspects of striving to be different.

To investigate the issue at hand, I had discussions with several entrepreneurs, seeking their opinions on what factors they feel make SME's stand out, from the standpoints of their own businesses and their suppliers. Several themes popped up common in all the conversations and I present them below.

Integrity

This is vital for the growth of any small businessperson and even for bigger businesses. People want to continually do business with suppliers and vendors they can trust not to hoodwink them.

One entrepreneur (Mr Chinedu) I spoke described this as having principles in business. He argued that this flows from the owner having the correct principles as a person and into the business. With time your clients (and your employees) will start recognizing these principles in the way the business is conducted. Chinedu insists on striving to run a value-driven business, where the business activities are driven by personal values.

My partner and I once purchased an earth-moving equipment from a dealer, Bawa, in Lagos that had some complications. After our inspection of the heavy-duty equipment, we noticed some abnormal noise from one of the gears under the equipment. The dealer, Bawa, assured us that it wasn't a big deal but just the gear cover, and he would get his parts supplier to replace before conveying the equipment to us in Port Harcourt.

We didn't feel too comfortable but we paid fully nonetheless and returned to Port Harcourt. The next day, Bawa called us from Lagos and told us that after investigations, he found out that the gear itself was bad and not just the cover. We started getting uneasy, but he assured us that our money would be returned and true to his word, by that evening he had wired the full amount back to our accounts.

Based on this experience, we became very comfortable doing business with Bawa and were quick to recommend him to other potential customers.

Businesses with integrity are quick to alert their customers when they have unknowingly overpaid or been overcharged. These businesses do not misrepresent their wares to customers.

For instance, an entrepreneur (Mr Kayode) dealing in agricultural products described to me how a young farmer reached out to him for help. The young farmer told Kayode that because of the coronavirus pandemic he had become stuck with a large stock of snails he had nurtured because it had become difficult to sell the products.

Mr Kayode asked for pictures from the farmer and received pictures of huge and well nurtured snails. But to his surprise, after completing the order for the products, he received completely different stock than what was represented in the pictures. Now Kayode is unwilling to have anything to do with that particular farmer, even after several apologies and pleadings.

Insisting on Quality

Entrepreneurs can stand out from rivals by ensuring the products they offer are consistently of high or higher quality. A businessperson I spoke to remarked that customers want the burden of always looking for quality products taken off their hands.

The example that this person gave was that of a vehicle spare parts dealer, who was able to differentiate himself from others in the spare parts market where he conducted business by always offering quality and original parts. So, his customers don't mind paying a bit more, as long as the burden of worrying about the originality and quality of parts they purchase is taken off their hands.

There was a building contractor that was awarded a job to construct one of many buildings for a government agency. The contractor insisted on delivering high quality, even going as far as demolishing some internal walls when they were done poorly and often clashing with the site engineer. As it happened, before the contractor could get his final payment for the job, a new management board was appointed to run the agency, replacing the management team that awarded these jobs.

On visiting the project sites, the management team was so impressed with the work this particular contractor had done, they decided to put the picture of the finished building on the face of their new magazine, showcasing their developmental efforts. The management also made sure the contractor was paid promptly, whilst cancelling the contracts of other shabbily done jobs. A lot of times, the quality of your output blows your trumpet.

Developing Personal Relationships

According to one entrepreneur, "person to person relationship strengthens bonds between businesses." He goes on to say, "You feel comfortable doing business with those you consider as friends, they can almost predict your attitude towards products and issues."

Building relationships with customers involves having what is commonly referred to as 'people skills.' Some businesspeople go out of the way to call clients, even when there is no ongoing business interaction, to say hello or extend wishes on birthdays and anniversaries.

Building personal relationships leads to long-term business relationships most of the times and customers always remember and value their long-term suppliers and vendors when considering doing new business.

Ensuring a Warm Reception

Everyone knows that you have to be friendly to customers when they walk into your establishment, but how come being treated warmly is a rare occurrence especially in small businesses. A lot of times customers are treated brusquely or rudely, when they walk into profit-making establishments, even in bigger businesses like banks, people are treated badly.

The universal law states that we should treat people, how we would like to be treated. When we are friendly, pleasant, helpful to customers, the customers in turn look to reward the business by patronizing and referring the organization or businessperson to others. Business owners must realize and act on this. Hire and train team members responsible for interacting with the public to display a warm attitude towards customers.

I recently visited a bank to request for a debit card, as my old one had expired. I really didn't need this card because I had a card from another account which was still valid, but I just thought I would have a second card for backup. One of the young ladies attending to customers, gave me a form and told me to sit and wait for my turn. I turned around and several people sitting down waiting but when I asked who had the last turn, they couldn't tell how their turns were being monitored.

After sitting for 30 minutes, I stood up and reminded the 'customer service' staff that it was just a card renewal I was there for. She curtly responded that it didn't matter, and I had to sit down and wait.

This got me thinking about whose interest it served that I renewed my debit card. Since, this card had expired I hadn't been charged 'card maintenance' fees and I was actually saving money. On the other hand, from these charges, the bank makes money and pays its staff members their salaries and bonuses. Once, I thought of it that way, I promptly closed my trap and walked out of the bank. The point I'm making is that businesses lose revenue when customers aren't treated well.

Creating Stickiness

This refers to offering value added services that your customers appreciate and these can convince them to continue their patronage. It is important that the customer regards the add-ons, or these won't be effective in keeping the customer's business. This is actually a competitive strategy (best cost strategy) but it's important, entrepreneurs keep it mind.

An example is when a sports equipment store offers golfers, free fitting or swing analysis services when they purchase new golf clubs. Most golfers will see this as valuable and such offers will go a long way to convince likely buyers. Or when an optician offers patients free eye tests to convince them to purchase glasses. As long as everyone else isn't offering the same value-added service, customer will appreciate these perks.

Conclusion/Key Takeaways

Small businesses more than often are not blessed with a lot of resources to embark on massive marketing/promotional campaigns or hire expensive consultants, yet they must find ways to stand out from their competitors. This chapter has presented several suggestions to the entrepreneur on how she can differentiate herself from the rest of the pile.

- Demonstrating integrity in dealing with customers should be a primary goal.

- Insisting on delivery quality every time will keep customers coming back again and again.

- Building personal relationships leads to long-term custom.

- Being friendly not only relieves stress but translates to profits for the business.

- Value-added services can be the honey for the trap.

Conclusion

It is not enough to read a book on entrepreneurship to be successful in business. You have to act on the knowledge you have gained, sometimes you might have to adapt or tweak some idea to fit your unique situation. This book is about thinking but also about action. It is now time for praxis – translating ideas into action.

In this book I espoused the importance in fine-tuning your strategy. You have to decide where your potential market lies and tailor your services and promotions to appeal to the members of this/these markets. Remember your segment could be based on geographical, demographic or behavioural characteristics or you probably want to serve a small select audience or niche.

You should probably do more research to understand the desires of the target market, this will help provide effective solutions to the problem you hope to address.

As you craft and implement your strategy, it is also your responsibility to take care of the bare-knuckle tactics of the venture i.e. the day to day operational procedures and issues that the business must carry on. These responsibilities include paying taxes and levies. I suggest keeping aside a percentage of revenues every month for taxes that will be paid when due, probably at the end of the year. Taxes SME's should be concerned about include: Company Income Tax, VAT, Withholding Tax, Education tax and Personal Income tax.

Entrepreneurs should also strive to build commitment amongst the team members. Employees that are highly committed are willing to go beyond what is expected of their job roles for the benefit of the organization. Committed employees improve the operational efficiency, provide better customer service and experience less stress in the workplace environment. Managers can focus on some areas to enhance commitment including designing effective rewards systems, crafting and articulating clear career growth/development paths, communicating effectively and consistently, leading by example and allowing for employee participation in the design and implementation of the long-term strategies as well as the job tasks.

Unfortunately, it is not always rosy for the entrepreneur or leader of the firm. Often, you will be faced with difficult situations. In some cases, marginal employees could create a negative environment in the workplace that could affect the operations of the organization and also the wellbeing of other members of the team. In this book, I have suggested several steps to deal with such difficult team members, including counselling and punishment.

Furthermore, we are often faced with crisis situations and it is not advisable to bury your head in the sand and hope for the best. I suggest deciding on a strategy to deal with the crisis, prioritizing the issues at hand and doing your best to preserve your mental wellbeing whilst dealing with the situation.

It is my sincere hope that this book provides solutions for the entrepreneur, leader, manager or supervisor.

Bibliography

1. Porter, Michael E. (1996) "What is Strategy?" *Harvard Business Review: November-December 1996* Online, Available from University of Liverpool/Laureate Online Education (Accessed on 5th November 2008).

2. Kotler P. and Keller K. (2009), "*Marketing Management*", 13th Edition, New Jersey, Pearson Custom Publishing.

3. Thompson A, Strickland A, Gamble J (2008); *Crafting and Executing Strategy. 16th Edition.* New York, McGraw-Hill Irwin.

4. Advanced English Dictionary (2020), "Tax, Taxation, Revenue Enhancement", Software Application IOS version 11.2.

5. Awoyemi, J. O., "Small and Medium Enterprises (SMEs) and its Tax Implications" http://wheretoprintmagazine.com/small-and-

medium-enterprises-smes-and-its-tax-
implication/.

6. Kotter, J. P. and Cohen, D. S. (2002), 'The Heart of Change: Real-life Stories of How People Change Their Organizations', Harvard Business School Press, Boston.

7. O'Reilly III, C. A. and Weitz, B. A. (1980), *'Managing Marginal Employees: The Use of Warnings and Dismissals'*, Administrative Science Quarterly, pp. 467-483, Vol. 25(3).

8. Freed, D. H. (2000), 'One More Time: Please Fire Marginal Employees', Health Care Manager, pp. 45-51, Vol. 18(3).

9. Knight, P. (2016), "Shoe Dog: A Memoir by the Creator of Nike", Simon & Schuster, London.

10. Cole, R. E. (2011), "Who Was Really at Fault for the Toyota Recalls", The Atlantic, https://www.theatlantic.com/business/archive/2011/05/who-was-really-at-fault-for-the-toyota-recalls/238076/.

11. Liker, J. (2011), "Toyota's Recall Crisis: What Have We Learned", Harvard Business Review, https://hbr.org/2011/02/toyotas-recall-crisis-full-of.

Acknowledgments

A lot of people have contributed to this book, to which I am eternally grateful to them. The list here is far from exhaustive but please blame it on my poor memory and not ingratitude.

I would like to give a special mention to Charles Okeibunor, who encouraged me and share so many ideas with me about so many topics. Also, my brother and business partner over many years, Omesuru. Our works together have been an inspiration for this book.

To the leaders and managers that agreed to participate in my research at different times., Ok Chike, Uloma Diriyai, Isioma Okiwelu, Philip Beke, Ozu Ake, Boma Obuforibo Jr., Vinnie Wokoma, Ikechukwu Odu, Kayode Ajileye, Chinedu Abanobi and Edward Inatimi. Thanks for your time and efforts.

It would be remiss of me not to mention the University of Liverpool Management School, my time there as an MBA and then DBA student can definitely not be measured. I came out with a treasure trove of knowledge.

To Nuhu Cheshi, for guiding me through the process of book publishing and encouraging me on this journey. Also, to the graphics team led by Chukwudera and his people. Your creativity is out of this world, I value your work more than I let on.

My appreciation goes to my great friends, Ernest Umeike, Gerald Ogbonna and Kalaina Okara for their advice on grammar and writing styles in general.

I would not have done this without my wife and kids, you guys were gracious and understanding enough to offer me the environment I needed to research and express my thoughts on paper, not to talk about the enthusiastic love I'm showered with on a daily basis.

About the Author

The author, Ukadike Ake, is a serial entrepreneur with forays into various sectors including entertainment, construction, equipment leasing, real estate and hospitality, all within a span of 25 years. He has experiences being an employee and an employer of labour.

He is the author of the book – Hit the Ground Running: How Start-ups can Start Right – which guides aspiring entrepreneurs into the world of starting businesses and getting it right from inception.

Ukadike Ake holds degrees in Engineering and Business Administration/Management including a Doctorate in Business Administration from the University of Liverpool. He has also conducted several training workshops in business skills including topics in business communications, managing change, team building and supervision.

He currently resides in Port Harcourt, Nigeria with his wife and kids. He's an avid golfer and passionately follows football and basketball.

www.ingramcontent.com/pod-product-compliance
Lightning Source LLC
Chambersburg PA
CBHW021450210526
45463CB00002B/715